Journey to the Sea Islands: Gullah Geechee Good!

Journey to the Sea Islands: Gullah Geechee Good!

Angel Brown Harriott

2019

Copyright © 2018 by Angel D. Harriott

All rights reserved. This book or any portion thereof may not be reproduced or used in any manner whatsoever without the express written permission of the publisher except for the use of brief quotations in a book review or scholarly journal.

First Printing: 2018
Second Edition

ISBN: 978-1-951881-01-6

Cultured Melanin Literary & Visual Arts Studios
44 Shipping Place
PO Box #4042
Baltimore, MD 21222
https://www.culturedmelanin.studio

www.globaljourneyforchildren.org
Phone: (301)910-7396

DEDICATION

This book is dedicated to my Grandmother, Ann Mariah Coles Mack (Leezie) who is one of the strongest women I ever knew and whom I admire, love and respect. I will never forget you and all that you poured into our family. *Sankofa*!

And to my Grandmother, Ethel Viola Brown (Humble Pie) who recently transitioned. Thank you for being a dedicated mother, grandmother, great grandmother & great, great grandma who cared for her family so lovingly and diligently. Thank you for our great talks and your funny stories while sharing our family history with me as I can now share it with others. *Sankofa*!

This book is dedicated to all of the queen mothers and fathers -generations of my family members who lived and persevered on John's Island, James Island and Wadmalaw Island, South Carolina to bring forward future generations who are still on the sea islands; or, those like me, who have become global children tied to states throughout America and other countries and continents around the world. We rest knowing that we come from the strong roots of the Gullah Tribe in Charleston, SC sea islands; and, that through your strength and perseverance, we thrive. *Sankofa*!

STAND
I stand on the shoulders of many
Many who fought for me
Many who stood up for me
Many who rose up for me
Many who even died for me

I am accountable to and have a responsibility for many who come behind me...
I have a responsibility to stand up for them, fight for them, RISE UP for them
having continued the quest
for humanity and equity for all.

Sya - 2016

"**You gotta have courage in order to step out and take a stand. Geechees have courage. We are strong-willed people.**"

Cousin Suzie Mae Simmons-Perry
Charleston, SC.

Table of Contents

DEDICATION V

ACKNOWLEDGEMENTS IX

PREFACE 1

JOURNEY TO THE SEA ISLANDS: GULLAH GEECHEE GOOD! 2

    Part 1: Homes and Landmarks of the Gullah People 2
    Part 2: Gullah Life 16
    The Angel Oak Tree 24
    Part 3: Gullah Legacies 28
    Great Blacksmiths of Charleston 29
    First Stop of the Transatlantic Slave Trade: West Indies 34
    Part 4: Gullah Champions 36
    Part 5: Gullah Elders 41
    Part 6: Growing up Gullah 45

REFERENCES 54

Acknowledgements

I would like to extend a special acknowledgement to my husband and sons for their ongoing love and support. Thank you for always being there and ready to lend a helping hand to support a cause that I am passionate about.

I would like to thank Venus Henry Vesey (US Navy) for sharing his family's historical journey with me to include in this book to share with the world. The entire section about Denmark Vesey is attributed to his great, great, great, great grandson, Venus H. Vesey, as told by elders from one generation to the next to maintain their family's experience and historical integrity.

Preface

           "Where are you from?"
Me: "South Carolina"
           "Which part?"
Me: " "Charleston"
           "Ooh, you're a Geechee...a Gullah Geechee"
           Laughter

For a very long time, Gullah people went unknown and unnoticed. The little which was known did not paint us in a positive light. It resulted in questions and commentary that were often disparaging rather than those that could enlighten. This caused many Gullah to try to change or deny who we were and to abandon some of our cultural traditions and language.

The Gullah people maintained our African history through their memory, knowledge and practice of customs and traditions from Africa. These traditions were passed down from one generation to the next, both intentionally and unintentionally. Through the research and work of several individuals and organizations, many people are now coming to understand and appreciate the history that they held onto for decades. This book pays homage to the Gullah Geechee people and includes my personal journey growing up Gullah in Charleston, SC and how I saw the world through my experience.

Journey to the Sea Islands: Gullah Geechee Good!

Part 1: Homes and Landmarks of the Gullah People

I grew up in Charleston, South Carolina. My family hails from the sea islands of Charleston. Some people call it the home of the Gullahs or Gullah Geechees. Charleston is also known as "the holy city" and "the low country". All of these names were given for different reasons. Many people believe that the term "Gullah" was an abbreviation for Africans who were brought to Charleston from Angola during the MAAFA (Transatlantic Slave trade). Instead of advertising the sale of Africans from Angola, ship captains referred to them as "Africans from Gola". This term eventually became known as "Gullah" to represent the captured Africans who were enslaved then taken to plantations along the sea island corridors of Charleston, South Carolina. There are many churches located throughout the city and surrounding area which is one reason it is called the holy city. I never heard that term until several years after I moved away. Finally, Charleston is located in a geographic region that is considered to be the low country area both for its flat land geography as well as its culture. It only takes a little rain to create floods in many of the streets in the city of Charleston because of its low-lying geography.

Charleston's sea islands have been proven to be one of the few places in the United States where there is a direct link to the continent of Africa based on African people who continued to practice their cultural traditions. Africans who lived there through the years were captured and brought there primarily from West Africa or they were later born to those captured African people.

The sea islands include the narrow coastal strip of land from Florida to Georgia and South Carolina up to the coastal area of North Carolina. My family has lived in Charleston and the sea islands for generations. My grandparents, great grandparents, great, great grandparents and great, great, great grandparents lived on John's Island, James Island and Wadmalaw Island in South Carolina on both my mother and father's side of the family. I guess you can say they were some of the original Gullah people. They certainly didn't plan it that way, it's just the way it came to be. So, Rosa, Margaret, Lavenia, Ann, Sila, Henrietta, Ethel, Charles, Louis, Nebuchadnezzar, Jerry, Richard, William, Henry, Leela, John, Aunt Sister, Edward, Della, Mena, Anna Lee, Betty, Junior, Sarah Lee, Bootsy, Thomas, Josephine (*Granny*) and our last elder, Susie Mack Rivers who transitioned at 102 years old, were family members who journeyed through those sea islands. According to historians and anthropologists, the Gullah people were discovered in Charleston's sea islands by missionaries in 1860. They returned to tell about the people they discovered in the New World with their own unique culture and language. Native Americans also lived on many of Charleston's sea islands during pre and post-colonial times. The current names of many cities and islands in Charleston, such as Kiawah and Edisto, reflects the names of some of those Native American tribes, whom some refer to as First Americans. Other Native American tribes in South Carolina included the Cusabo, Stono, Ashepoo, Edisto, Kiawah and Coosa just to name a few.

From 1670 to 1808, about 122,000 Africans were brought from Senegal through Angola; and, 76% of slaves in SC were African born in 1740. This does not include the captured Africans who were brought after enslavement was declared illegal.

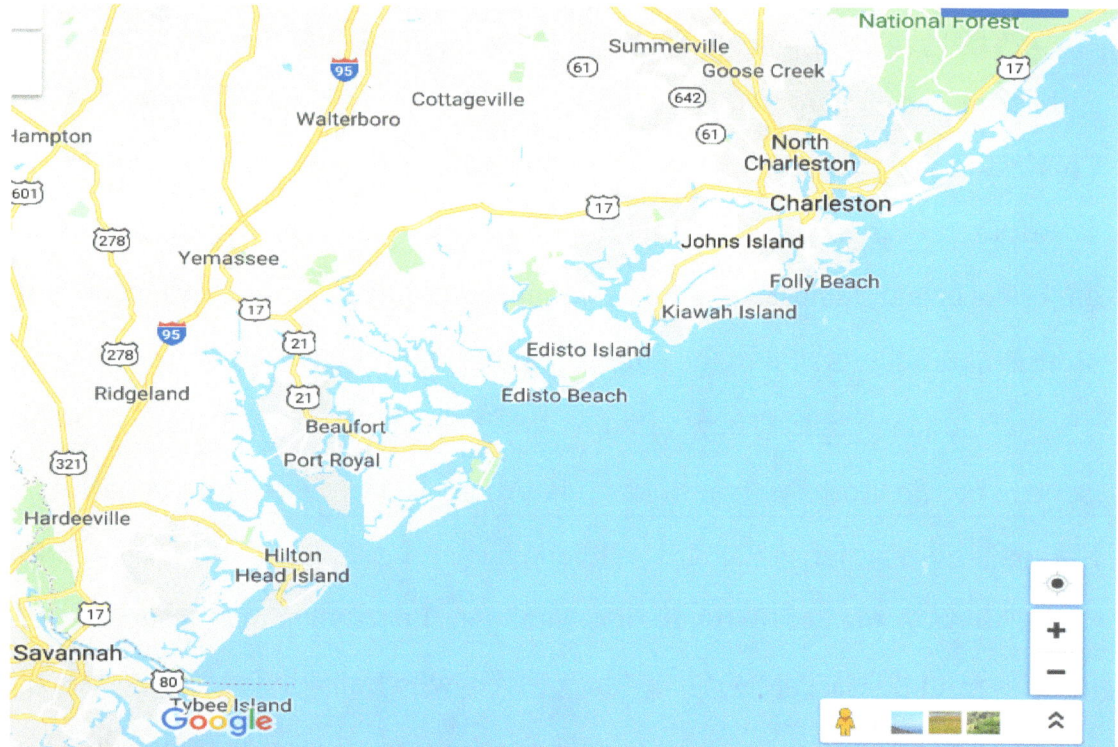

Sea Islands along the coast of Charleston, SC   Map data ©Google

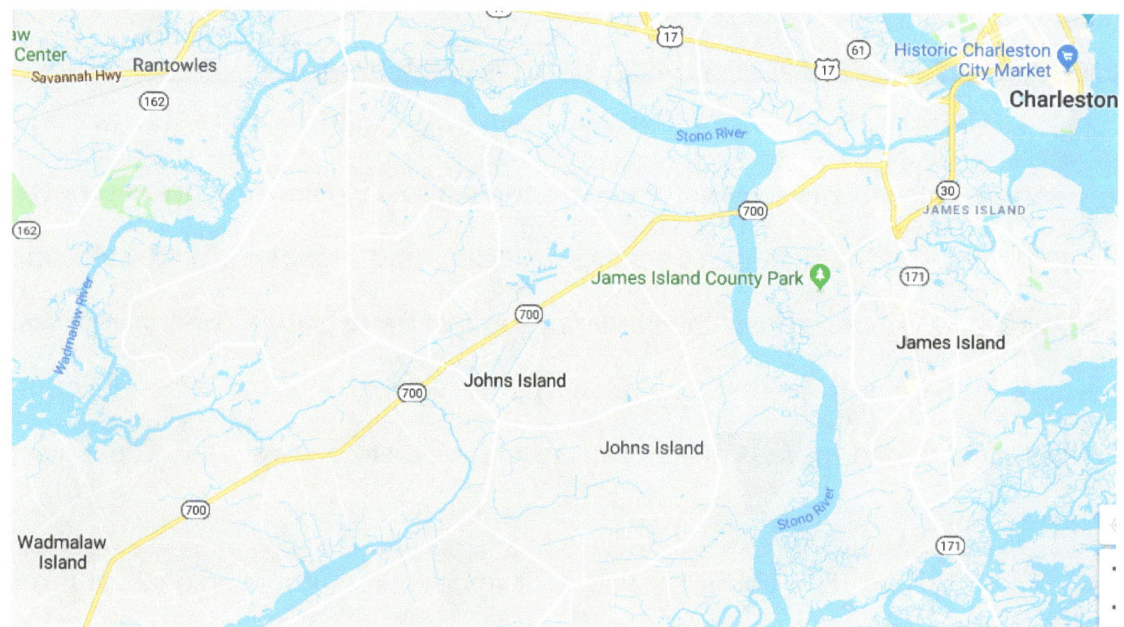

Sea Islands where my family lived in Charleston   Map data ©Google

Upon arrival to Charleston, the ancestors of many African American people worked on plantations like the one pictured below. These plantations all had a large main house where owners of the enslaved people lived. The photo below is a rearview of McLeod Plantation which was built in 1851 on James Island, SC. Some plantations, such as Magnolia Plantation, are even older – built in 1676.

©GJFC, Inc. 9/2018

© GJFC, Inc. 9/2018

The photograph above is the front view of the main house on McLeod Plantation. Ironically, a plantation house was called the "white house". Four months after taking this photograph, I learned that my family members actually lived on this plantation. It was informative yet uncomfortable to be there during the early research; but, it was even more disturbing to learn that information later.

While captors, or owners of plantations, lived in the main house with their families, captured Africans lived in one room houses that were called slave quarters. They looked like the one pictured below and on the following pages. These are not replicas. They are houses where captured and enslaved African families actually lived. These houses were small rooms where no one had separate bedrooms or a family room, kitchen or even a bathroom.

Inside one room cabin at McLeod Plantation, James Island, SC ©GJFC, Inc. 9/2018

McLeod Plantation, James Island, SC ©GJFC, Inc. 9/2018

My family lived in one of the last white cabins that still stands on McLeod Plantation today. They did not have running water or electricity. Like the other families, they had to use an open chimney to cook meals for the family and for heat.

Point of Pines Plantation, Edisto Island, SC

The cabin above, known to be on the Point of Pine plantation since 1851, was donated to the National African American Museum of History and Culture (NAAMHC) in Washington, DC. It is one of the oldest slave quarters (cabins for enslaved people) that has been preserved in the United States of America. Now, you can go to the NAAMHC Museum to see this cabin and think about how the people must have felt living in this space. It also helps us all to remember their existence and their journey.

Captured Africans were frequently sold in places like the "Old Slave Mart" pictured below. It is now a museum in downtown Charleston. It is a sad but powerful reminder of how African people were treated during that time. It shows the small spaces where they were forced to stay until families or individual family members were sold at auction. Children were often separated from their parents and sold to the highest bidders. This represented the beginning of the intentional breakdown of African families.

Old Slave Mart Museum © GJFC, Inc. 9/2018

As a child, I visited many of the sea islands in South Carolina, like John's Island, Edisto Island, Wadmalaw Island and later James Island where my grandparents lived while I was growing up. My family members and family friends could be easily found residing on any of those islands, so going there to visit or stay with relatives on any or all of them was second nature to me.

For my parents, their siblings and close relatives, spending time or living on the sea islands was a way of life. It was a part of the culture even after they moved away to live in the city. My uncle Arnold and cousin Theresa tell stories about how the elders gathered all of the children every fifth Sunday and took them to the country, a reference to the sea islands. They prepared a basket full of food and they had a time of fellowship at church so they could meet their relatives who still lived on John's Island and Wadmalaw Island. This was an important part of maintaining family ties, culture and familiarity with traditions. This was a way to practice those traditions, tell and hear stories and to know where you could go and stay if there was a need. It was going back to your home place and back to your roots.

If I close my eyes, I can still see the beauty of the islands. I see big, tall beautiful trees that swayed gently across the blue Carolina sky. The air was always thick and wet with hot and humid summer breezes, even during the Spring and Fall. Some of the trees were wrapped in vines that had grown tightly around the barks and branches throughout the years. Many of them still have Spanish moss draping through the leaves and across the branches today. There were no street lamps on most of the island so it was very dark and quiet at night except for the sounds of crickets singing.

The Landscape of Charleston and the Sea Islands

© GJFC, Inc. 9/2018

Oak trees with Spanish moss may be found throughout many of the sea islands.

John's Island is but one of the few places referred to as a "sea island' along the southeastern coastline. It stretches across a coastal strip of land that is about 250 miles long and about 40 miles wide. This small island and others like it, which was separate from the city of Charleston, was considered to be hot, rural marshlands with little to no value. That was in the beginning. That was before early European colonists determined that Africans could be used as a commodity to increase the value of those marshlands by using their skill and expertise in planting, growing and harvesting cotton and rice.

Marshlands in Charleston, South Carolina

Coastal lines of John's Island, South Carolina.   © GJFC, Inc., 9/2018

The photograph above shows present day Charleston with connecting bridges to some of the sea islands. If you look at the photograph and imagine the bridges removed, you might have an idea of how the Gullah people lived disconnected from the rest of the people in the city of Charleston. This disconnection from the city and lack of interruptions from European colonists helped the Gullah people because they were able to continue practicing their own cultural traditions without outside influences. That is how Gullah people preserved their language, religion, music, arts and crafts, agricultural skills and overall way of life for so long.

Part 2: Gullah Life

Many of the Africans who were forced to come to America to work as enslaved people were brought to the port of Charleston from Africa and the West Indies. Some of the first Africans brought to Charleston from the West Indies were from Barbados. Upon arrival, they were eventually taken to the sea islands to work on farms and plantations. These were the first of the African people who would eventually come to be known as "Gullah" people. Through the years they were also often referred to as "Gullah Geechee" or "Geechees" depending on where they were living along the sea island coast.

After these captured African people were granted their liberty (by President Abraham Lincoln's executive order, Emancipation Proclamation 95 on January 1, 1863), some of them went to Liberia (which means liberty), a small country in West Africa near Sierra Leone. Others remained isolated on the sea islands as a village community for many years. Many of the plantations had been burnt down and the owners fled to the city and other places. There were no bridges or overpasses that brought people from the city to these islands. Even prior to Emancipation, European colonists found themselves ill-equipped to handle the heat and humidity or the diseases, such as malaria, that came along with living on the sea islands. Africans were accustomed to this climate and had worked in it for thousands of years in Africa. As a result of heat and diseases, plantation owners moved back into the city of Charleston, or they lived in the city during the hot months and left one or more of their enslaved Africans to oversee, or manage, the plantation.

They continued practices such as farming, quilting, making fishing nets, and knitting sweet grass baskets. Some of my family members still weave sweetgrass baskets. They are among the few people who sell their goods at the Old Charleston Market. Those baskets and other decorative items made from sweetgrass are considered to be extremely valuable pieces of Charleston's cultural identity. Even the smallest basket and other kinds of items that they now weave are priced to reflect the value of that distinction. Most sweetgrass basket weavers will only pass this skill to family members. This craft goes back to Africa where they used baskets in practical ways, such as storing and carrying items or winnowing (sifting) rice with coil baskets. They also continued traditions that honored their ancestors by practicing funerary songs and dances passed down by their ancestors. They were undisturbed. This isolation was a gift that allowed for the preservation of a people that would one day be observed and used by Lorenzo Dow Turner. Dr. Turner was an African American linguist (person who studied languages) who did his research on the Gullah language. His research was an important link to connecting these African people living in village communities found along the sea island coast back to African people living in Sierra Leone, West Africa.

There have been many others who have contributed to the early research of Gullah culture, such as Dr. Emory Campbell, Executive Director of the Penn Center on St. Helena Island in South Carolina and Dr. Joseph Opala, an American anthropologist and historian. They helped many Gullah people visit Sierra Leone, West Africa where they met and bonded with people in African villages who shared the same customs, language and traditions that they had practiced for years.

GJFC, Inc.9/2018

African women made sweetgrass baskets for thousands of years. The same sweetgrass baskets were made by Gullah women in Charleston's sea islands when they arrived and they continue to be created by Gullah people along the Southeast corridor. They are most often referred to as "Sweetgrass Basket Ladies". Each family has their own pattern to identify themselves as the basket maker.

©Photo By K. Owusu, 12/2018

This quilt, donated by Baba Kojo Owusu, is estimated to be 95 years old. It was given to him by his Grandmother, who received it from her Great Grandmother. They both resided in South Carolina. Quilts were made from several different pieces of materials and the patterns in them served many different purposes. They kept our ancestors warm and they were used to communicate hidden messages, such as identifying escape routes for enslaved Africans seeking to rebel.

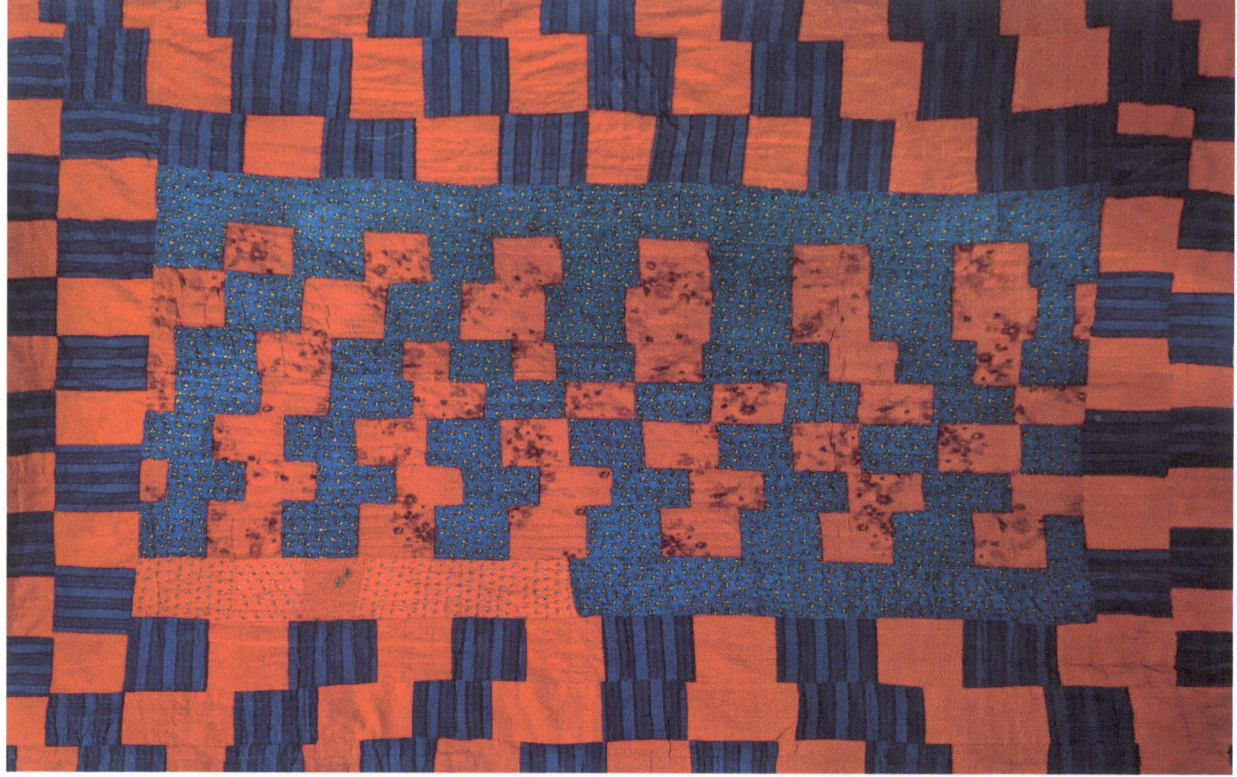

©Photo By GJFC, Inc., 12/2019

This quilt, given to me by my aunt and uncle, belonged to my Grandma Leezie. She grew up on the sea islands (Johns Island) in South Carolina. You will notice that this quilt is completely different from the quilt on page 19. If you look closely, you will see one block with two sea turtles. Sea turtles were commonly found on the beaches in the sea islands and even today, they continue to nest their eggs there. I feel the warmth of my grandma when I spread this quilt around me.

Today's Gullah people are the generations of descendants born to captured Africans who remained on the land after they were freed from bondage. Some of the Gullah people's children (freed Africans who were later called negroes, Blacks and African Americans), migrated north to make a better life. My grandma, Leezie, was one of those people who went to New York City to find work that would help to support the family. There were thousands of others who found their way north to earn money for their families because the conditions were better for them there but they were far from ideal. This was known as the Great Migration. They still had challenges in the northern states.

For many years prior to Emancipation and some years afterward, Charleston relied upon sea island cotton and rice as its main source of wealth. When "King Cotton" was no longer king because the price of cotton went down, some Gullah people who did not migrate north moved from the islands to the city to work. Some did domestic work while others used trade skills to become entrepreneurs. They began to create their own financial resources and institutions and they created communities where they became homeowners and entrepreneurs. Some eventually worked in shipyards, like my grandfather, a US Marine, who worked at the Navy Shipyard where I had one of my first jobs as a teenager. Others worked at factories that were located downtown in the city of Charleston.

The Gullahs who remained on the islands took over the plantations. They were able to stay on the land due to "Sherman's Field Order No. 15". In 1865, after Sherman's March to the Sea (also called the Savannah Campaign) and after meeting with several black leaders, Union General William Tecumseh Sherman issued an order requiring land and abandoned rice fields from south Charleston to Florida for

30 miles back from the sea to be given to Africans to settle. This is the order from where the well-known phrase "40 acres and a mule" was taken. The order was supposed to allow recently freed "negroes" to stay on the land they had worked for so many years and generations. Unfortunately, many of them had to return the land to their original owners after President Andrew Johnson was elected in 1865.

President Andrew Johnson was the 17th president of the United States of America. He overturned Sherman's Order so the Africans (referred to as negroes in the order) had no choice but to return the land to the original plantation owners. The little progress made would soon be taken away much like the right to vote that was granted in 1867 when the Africans became "freedmen". This was the first time they were able to participate in the political system. This changed abruptly in 1890 and was followed by Jim Crow laws leading to segregation. Those laws negatively affected the rights of African Americans to have access to educational resources, voting rights, employment and land ownership. Those Africans who were able to keep their land after Sherman's Order eventually passed it down to future generations by a term known as "heir's property". Heirs property describes land that was given to former enslaved Africans after the civil war. The land is owned by two or more family members of an ancestor who did not have a will or the land did not have a deed of ownership so it was passed to other family members from one generation to the next generation informally. This was a common practice on Charleston's sea islands as well as those along the entire southeast coast where Gullah people inhabited the land.

Cherry Point, John's Island, SC where my family lived. © GJFC, Inc. 9/2018

The Angel Oak Tree

Many of the sea islands in Charleston have similar geography. They were all near the water, all low-lying communities and all rural with wildlife and forestry that had grown for hundreds of years before colonization. However, one of the trees on John's Island is known throughout the world. It is a huge live oak tree called the "Angel Oak". The Angel Oak tree is considered to be one of the oldest trees in the United States. It is estimated to be more than 1,000 years old. It is a massive tree that stands about 65 feet tall and about 25 feet wide. The tree branches are so big and long that they look like they are reaching out to you from all directions. They are so long and heavy that some of the branches lay on the ground and others appear to be buried and rising through the earth for a second time. Diverse people from around the world who tour Charleston come to visit this tree which has been designated as a national treasure.

Angel Oak Tree © GJFC, Inc. 9/2018

© GJFC, Inc. 9/2018

The Angel Oak tree was designated as the 2004 National Heritage Tree by the South Carolina Urban and Community Forestry Council.

© GJFC, Inc. 9/2018

Like the Angel Oak, many of the trees on John's Island are very old and they seem to tell a story of their own. As I drove down the long roads peering out at the thick forests, I thought of my ancestors and wondered about their journey through this land. I thought of earlier generations working in the fields and imagined their longing to be free in what was an unfamiliar place and continent. I think of later generations toiling in the field to make a living and of those who had to leave the family behind to earn money in other cities in order to care for the family.

Can you imagine how many stories the Angel Oak tree could tell if it could talk? It would have seen my ancestors and maybe some of yours from hundreds of years ago when they were brought to the port in Charleston and as they first arrived on John's Island and Wadmalaw Island from Africa and the West Indies.

© GJFC, Inc. Photos by S. Wright 1/2019

Photo of Gadsen's Wharf in Charleston.

© GJFC, Inc. Photos by S. Wright 1/2019

Gadsens Wharf was built by Christopher Gadsen in the mid 1700s. This Port was the destination for thousands of Africans who were brought to Charleston. It was the only place where ships could bring their cargo of kidnapped African people during the last two years of the legal slave trade ending in 1807. However, many Africans were still captured and forced into enslavement illegally after that date.

Part 3: Gullah Legacies

There is a lot of African history throughout Charleston, South Carolina beyond the sea islands. Before the American Revolutionary Wars were fought from 1775 to 1783, Charleston was called "Charles Town." It was under British rulers. African labor was used to create wealth throughout South Carolina by the sales of products and goods they grew, such as cotton and rice, or "King Cotton" and "Carolina Gold Rice". They were given those names because of the massive wealth the products accumulated for European colonists. Africans farmed for thousands of years before being taken from Africa and brought to the United States, specifically South Carolina, to grow and harvest rice. Their skills were highly desirable to support the new crop in South Carolina. My great grandparents eventually owned a rice farm and cotton farm, along with other crops they grew on Johns and James Island.

Africans produced rice for over 3,000 years in places like Mali, Songhai and Ghana.

Great Blacksmiths of Charleston

Gullah people were also skilled iron makers, brick layers, carpenters and welders who used the concept of apprenticeships to pass on their skills to the next generation. It was their skills and labor that was also used to build many of the structures that are still standing throughout the city of Charleston today. They also used those skills and trades to become entrepreneurs.

One well known blacksmith who has touched the lives of many Charlestonians through the years and whose work may be found throughout the entire city of Charleston is Phillip Simmons. He created beautiful gates and decorative ironworks that may be found on historical buildings, government buildings, balconies, churches and residential homes, including some of my family's homes. The place where he mastered his craft never changed through the years. It still stands today and his apprentice, nephew Carlton Simmons, continues the tradition as demonstrated by the Sankofa symbol he welded for us as we watched. Mr. Simmons was a well-known and respected blacksmith in Charleston and in the United States. Around my house, he was simply and lovingly called "Simmons" during his many chats or visits with my parents.

The city of Charleston recognized the life and contributions of Phillip Simmons by erecting a statue of him in Phillip Simmons Park on the East Side of Charleston. There is also a foundation that continues to document his ironworks and educate the public about his contributions.

Statue of Phillip Simmons   ©GJFC, Inc. 9/2018

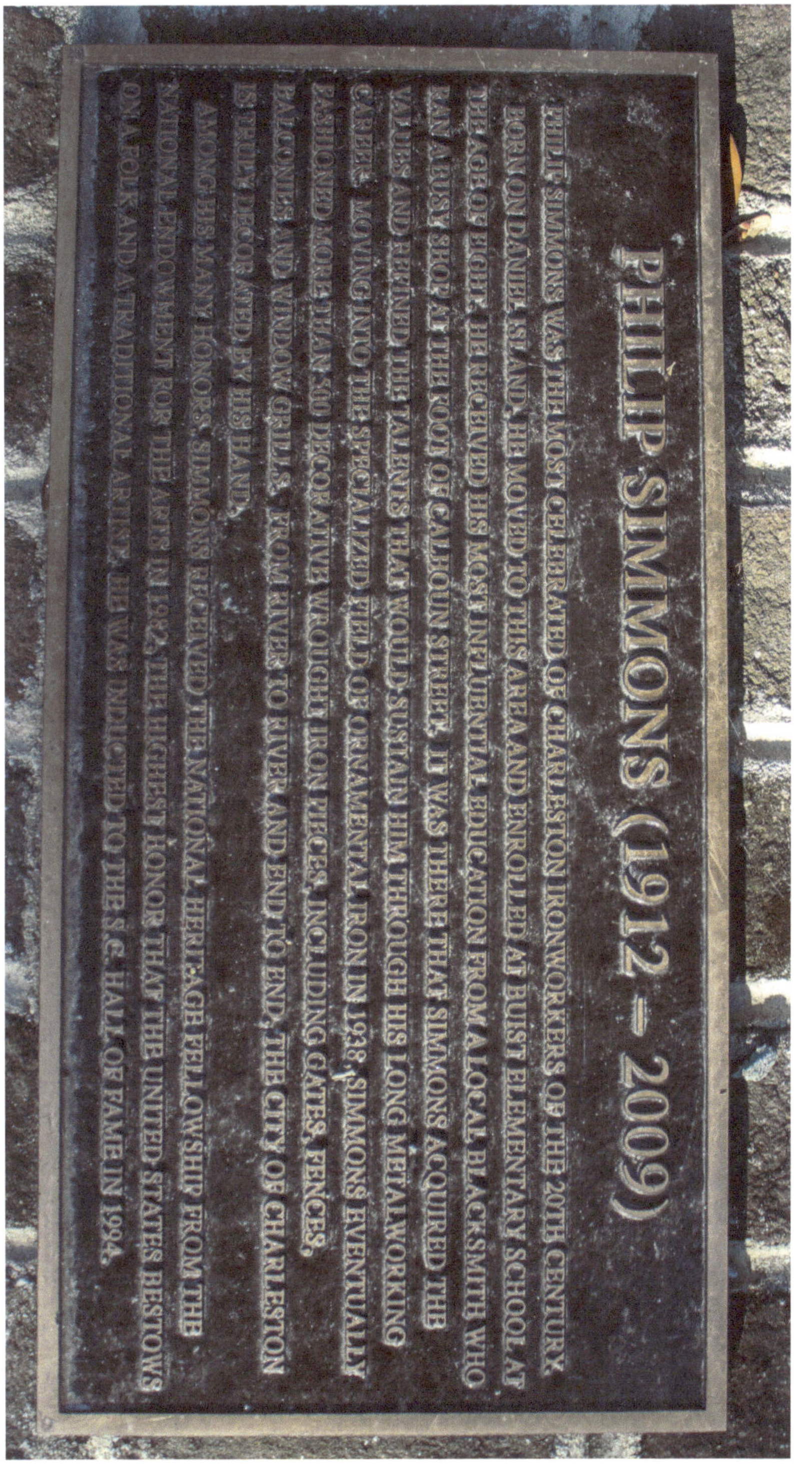

PHILIP SIMMONS (1912 – 2009)

Philip Simmons was the most celebrated of Charleston ironworkers of the 20th century. Born on Daniel Island, he moved to this area and enrolled at Buist Elementary School at the age of eight. He received his most influential education from a local Black smith who ran a busy shop at the foot of Calhoun Street. It was there that Simmons acquired the skills and refined the talents that would sustain him through his long metal working career. Moving into the specialized field of ornamental iron in 1938, Simmons eventually fashioned more than 500 decorative wrought iron pieces, including gates, fences, balconies and window grills, from river to river and end to end, the City of Charleston is richly decorated by his hand.

Among his many honors, Simmons received the National Heritage Fellowship from the National Endowment for the Arts in 1982, the highest honor that the United States bestows on a folk and traditional artist. He was inducted to the S.C. Hall of Fame in 1994.

Plaque for Phillip Simmons

©GJFC, Inc. 9/2018

Photo of Carlton Simmons, nephew and apprentice of Phillip Simmons, forging a Sankofa symbol. If you look closely, you will see this Adinkra symbol in ironworks throughout Charleston and many other cities and states!

©GJFC, Inc. 9/2018

Carlton Simmons works in the shop where Phillip Simmons trained him. He has received distinguished awards for his mastery as a blacksmith.

©GJFC, Inc. 9/2018

A finished Sankofa symbol crafted for Global Journey for Children, Inc.

First Stop of the Transatlantic Slave Trade: West Indies

Many of the Africans who were kidnapped from West Africa were taken to the West Indies first. Later, they were brought to Charleston, SC from Barbados, Jamaica and many other islands in the West Indies. They did similar work in the West Indies but they were primarily taken there to work in the sugar fields, or on sugar plantations. The wealth producing commodity in the West Indies was sugar. Today, you can still see the aged sugar mills that were used to create sugar.

During a recent visit, I was able to see the old aqua-duct system that was created to carry water as a part of the process for making sugar. The enslaved Africans used an aqua-duct system that turned a large wooden wheel to carry water across a bridge. It operated like a mechanical system that squeezed the sugar cane to extract the juice. The juice was placed into a copper pot and put on fire inside of a sugar mill like the one pictured on the following page. They boiled the sugar cane juice to crystallize it. This made it turn into a hardened form, which is the sugar you see packaged in a grocery store.

Documented records show that an estimated 6, 676 enslaved Africans were brought from the West Indies and 114,788 were brought from Africa to Charleston. This helps to explain why there are so many similarities in the traditions and speech of Gullah people and people from the West Indies. The "Gullah" dialect may be heard in both the Caribbean islands and the sea islands of Charleston, SC and the remaining sea islands along the southeast coastline. It is very similar to the "Krio" language spoken by Africans in Sierra Leone, West Africa.

Sugarmill in Jamaica © GJFC, Inc. 9/2018

An old sugar mill sits abandoned in the Ironshore community of Jamaica. It was formerly a sugar cane plantation. It is located on Sugar Mill Road. After the decline in the production of sugar, some of the sugar plantations were turned into banana plantations and Jamaica became a primary source for bananas. One of the first families to own a sugar plantation was the Barnett family in Jamaica. A main street is named Barnett Street for that family's legacy.

Part 4: Gullah Champions

There were many attempts to rebel and runaway by enslaved and free blacks in the West Indies and Charleston. Angolans in SC revolted in 1739. Some were successful but some attempts to runaway failed. One such attempt was called the "Uprising".

Around 1781-1782, Captain Joseph Vesey arrived in Charleston accompanied by an enslaved boy named Denmark Vesey. Captain Vesey took a fancy to this young boy whom he had previously sold to a planter in the Virgin Islands. In 1781, Vesey transported 390 slaves to St. Dominique. Among his cargo was a 14-year old boy who had been living on St. Thomas. Captain Vesey sold him to a French planter for a high price. Three months later he became ill and the planter demanded a refund. Captain Vesey repurchased the boy and decided to keep him as his own property. Vesey named him Denmark because he had been part of the shipment from the Danish Colony of St. Thomas. Vesey's family is unclear whether he was born in Africa or on the island of St. Thomas in the Caribbean. What is certain is that he was living on St. Thomas by the time he was 14 years old.

When the Captain got Denmark back again, he used him as a cabin boy. Denmark became the captain's personal slave and began sailing with him throughout the Caribbean and along the African coast. From 1781 to 1783, Denmark saw all of the activities of the slave trading world. During the journey from Africa, it was told that the smell of human waste, disease and death was so strong that it often overwhelmed Denmark.

Captain Vesey actually raised Denmark and he educated him. Denmark could converse in many languages. In 1783, Captain Joseph Vesey gave up the slave trade and settled in Charleston, South Carolina because it was the fourth largest city in America and it had a busy harbor at the Ashley and Cooper rivers. This location made it an ideal place for his business dealing in ship supplies. While living in Charleston with Captain Vesey, four free blacks and an East Indian woman, Denmark became an apprentice carpenter and had opportunities he would not have had as an enslaved African working on a plantation. On the street corners of Charleston, he was exposed to people who enjoyed exchanging opinions on current issues. He also held discussions with other slaves and free blacks.

In December 1799, Denmark won the lottery for $1,500. He asked Captain Vesey to buy his freedom, informing him that he had the cash available. The captain set the price at $600 and scheduled the sale to take place the following month. So, in January 1800, Denmark met Captain Vesey in the library on a quiet winter evening. He gave his master $600 and in return received his manumission papers at the age of 33 years old. With the rest of his money, Denmark bought himself a house on Bull Street and joined the small community of free blacks that lived in the city of Charleston. As a free black he had to be careful to carry his manumission papers with him at all times. Even though these papers proved his status as a free man, they failed to provide him with any legal guarantee that he would not be abducted and sold back into slavery.

Once Denmark was free, he sought a way to free others from slavery. Denmark believed that this was wrong. He visited with Richard Allen, the founder of the African Methodist Episcopal (AME) Church in Pennsylvania. Allen was a pioneer in creating the first recognized black denomination in the US. He came back to organize with other blacks and they eventually built Mother Emmanuel Church, one of the oldest black church congregations in the south where African Americans could worship independently. Unfortunately, the church was closed then burned down. As a result, many of the free and enslaved people came together and elected Denmark Vesey as the leader to help them obtain their freedom.

Denmark began to read abolitionist pamphlets and followed the news from St. Domingue about a slave revolt that in 1804 led to the formation of a black republic. St. Domingue was a small island in the Caribbean that was under French rule. Captured Africans were brought there to work on plantations for the export of sugar and coffee. After a massive slave rebellion which led to a revolution, slaves won their freedom on January 1, 1804. They renamed the island, Haiti, as it is presently called today. Vesey was convinced that blacks would gain their freedom in America only through similar bloodshed, so he began organizing a similar uprising in South Carolina.

In June 1822, the Charleston militia crushed Vesey's rebellion just hours before it was to take place. One of his men informed authorities about the planned rebellion. Vesey was convicted of raising an insurrection and was hanged at the

age of 55, along with many enslaved Africans. The conspiracy succeeded in terrifying slave owners and dividing the nation on the emancipation issue. With his bold stance on black rights, Denmark Vesey had fanned the flames that later blazed into a civil war. The city of Charleston started a military school, called the The Citadel, to help prevent another rebellion spearheaded by captured African people who desired and fought for their freedom.

Denmark's family journey began in Africa to Bermuda, St. Thomas to Southeastern USA (via Charleston, SC) to Texas. His living great, great, great, great grandson, Venus Henry Vesey, continues to tell his family story for future generations. The Vesey family would go on to fight in the Civil War, WWI, WWII, Iraq War, Korean War, Vietnam, and Desert Storm on behalf of the USA. They also fought as volunteers in the Spanish American War as African American veterans under Theodore Roosevelt in an effort to liberate Cuba from Spain. Denmark's son, Robert Vesey, helped to raise the flag at Fort Sumter when the US Army reclaimed it after the Civil War. Like his father, Robert was a carpenter, so he also helped to rebuild the Mother Emmanuel Church which meant so much to the African American community.

Statue of Denmark Vesey. It is presently located in Hampton Park.

Part 5: Gullah Elders

My family eventually owned land on Mullet Hall which is located on John's Island, James Island and Cherry Point which is located on Wadmalaw Island. My family elders tell stories about our great, great, great grandparents who grew fruit trees, cow peas, beans, watermelon, rice and cotton. They recall how they were called to harvest the fruits and vegetables they grew much like I was when I was a young girl. They grew food to eat and food to sell as produce which was the main way they supported our family at that time.

My grandma (Humble Pie) told me stories about our great, great, great grandma who was a midwife, which means she delivered babies for women in the John's Island community and she helped care for the new mothers. She smiled as she told me stories that she remembered about her grandmother wearing beautiful braids. She patted her head as she talked about how our great, great grandma's beautiful braids were piled high on the top of her head like a crown with some type of tassels on top. That surely sounds like a beautiful African woman to me!

Humble Pie's father (our great grandfather) was a postal mailman who delivered mail throughout John's Island. My grandmother smiles as she reminisces on how often she sat in the back seat of his car while he delivered the mail. He would tell her to dive into the backseat and relax while he delivered mail throughout his territory in the country. She had so much fun as they drove down the long winding roads which eventually led to a dead-end and a hill; but, she was delighted when they would finally reach the curve at the end of his mail route. Once there, she would gaze at the large entry gate that led to Kiawah Island on one side and a big plantation on the other side.

Kiawah Island, SC, originally owned by Kiawah Native Americans

People who lived on or visited Kiawah Island enjoyed its white sandy beaches that touched the Atlantic Ocean. Grandma longed to enter those gates and have a chance to collect some of the beautiful sea shells. When she was a little older, she finally managed to get through those gates to see Kiawah Island. She had her chance to go there with Josephine Bunno, a neighbor who was visiting a friend on the island. Once there she saw those sea shells she had always heard about. There were so many of them scattered throughout the sand that she didn't know where to start. She soon learned that it was not all fun and games. On the way to the beach, there were roads with many branches. Grandma didn't know that there were fleas on those branches. Great grandma had to scour her body and hair to remove them.

I smiled as Grandma fondly recalled when she finally visited Kiawah Island. She sat at the kitchen table with us and giggled throughout her storytelling. "Wen I get home, my mama took de wick off duh lamp an said "chil you loaded wid fleas!" From dat time on, I said I don't care how beautiful it is, I ain't never goin back dere no more and I ain't never went back no more neither!" After we all laughed hysterically, she went on to finish her story.

"You go ta dat gate, but wen ya get but a few steps dey den ya gotta have some kind a papus in order ta go all de way. I remembuh a few years back, I went ta take one uh dem boys ta show'em and man …I couldn't even get ova dere. Dey say if you go you gotta go through dat same gate and dis lady always sittin at duh desk askin fuh papus. Man, I say I ain't got no papus."

Kiawah Island was an exclusive island. Each person who wanted to visit the island was required to show a pass that would allow them to enter through the gate. Even today, Kiawah Island is not open to the pubic without the required pass. This land got its name from the Native Americans called Kiawah, who originally lived on and owned the land.

Kiawah Island's point of entry as it stands today. © GJFC, Inc.-9/2018

Part 6: Growing up Gullah

When I was a little girl, I remember my parents taking me to visit my family on John's Island and Wadmalaw Island. Sometimes, I would help in the fields. This was often not our choice but we were volunteered for duty by my parents. "Why don't you let those girls help out?" is what I would hear my Mom say before we were led to the outdoors. I didn't necessarily want to go but I knew better than to let that thought escape my head through my mouth.

Beyond the small house with the wooden porch and three little wooden stairs, there was a field of different vegetables growing for what looked like miles and miles from my young eyes. I don't remember which types anymore. I only remember that it was burning hot and we had to go outside into the field to pick those vegetables. Once we began to harvest them, work turned into silly playful games as we gathered the vegetables. We laughed, ran, skipped and played until suddenly, work didn't seem like work at all. Instead, we had so much fun as we picked those vegetables that we hardly realized we were working and also learning about agriculture. It was simply Gullah Geechee Good!

There wasn't a lot to do in this very rural island. There were no parks with basketball courts, baseball fields, tennis centers or even community centers. There were often many miles between stores or neighbors, unless groups of family members had houses on the same property. There were no internet, Nintendo, Xbox or PlayStation games. So, we had to be creative. Children used their imaginations and we made our own fun. We blew bubbles made of soap and water. We jumped rope or played hopscotch. We played ball or sometimes we played hide and go seek for hours. We also played with our jackstones on the

porch when we remembered to bring them with us. I especially remember getting sugar canes and chewing on them to taste the sweetness of the sugar. I imagine that most children today wouldn't know how a sugar cane looked if it jumped on them and bit down hard!

© GJFC, Inc. 9/2018

    Pictured above are sugarcanes. These ones were actually grown in Jamaica. On the left is how the cane appears when harvested. On the right, the cane has been peeled. Many people chop the cane and eat it after it has been peeled. This is how I was taught to eat it growing up Gullah in the sea islands also.

As I grew older, and especially when I visited other places, I remember being called a Gullah, Geechee or Gullah Geechee. Most of the time if someone called you one of those names it was because of where you came from and how the people were known to speak. Sometimes, it was a disparaging remark based on the limited knowledge people had about Gullah life. The Gullah language is usually spoken fast and all of the words were not in the English dictionary. It was a combination of languages and words that were strung together and spoken rapidly which made it difficult for strangers to understand. Most people thought it was plain old bad English. It was actually a language born out of necessity.

African people spoke different languages depending on what tribe or country they were from in Africa. When they were brought to America, their captors spoke English. The Gullah people were actually quite smart when you think about it because some of them had to learn a new language which they eventually mixed in with some of their own native words from Africa. Some Africans knew English words, especially if they were from the West African region where they spoke Creole. The Creole language was a combination of African words and English that was spoken by many different African tribes. They were able to understand and communicate with the captors on the plantation and they were able to maintain their own language to talk among each other. Sometimes plantation owners tried to change this by grouping people from different countries in Africa together so they would not be able to communicate with each other. This was done to separate the captured African people and to reduce the chance for them to plan an escape or rebellion. They still found ways to communicate and work together for freedom.

I grew up hearing both English and Gullah. Neither language seemed right or wrong; they were just different so I was comfortable with both. I enjoyed hearing my family tell stories in Gullah. Their stories sounded colorful and fun. They often included all sorts of facial expressions, sounds and body movements to illustrate their stories. Our family elders always had a way of telling a story like a folklore to make a point when they were teaching children.

Our ancestors used this same type of language to pass secret messages in stories or songs, like folklores and old "spiritual" songs. Sometimes it was to make themselves feel better or stronger to get through the harsh times and other times it was to give praise to God. Gullah people are a spiritual people and you could see our strong ties to spirituality when you visit praise houses where they worshipped. This is still a sacred practice that is demonstrated and taught by families and cultural preservationist, Marquette Goodwine, known as Chieftess Queen Quet, a leading voice of the Gullah people and community. Today, she continues to educate people through her organization. She travels the world to speak about the importance of maintaining the land, culture and traditions of Gullah people.

When I visited my family on the sea islands, there were some things that were very different from my daily existence. Sometimes I think about it and I smile and other times I frown. I can still recall the awful taste of the water. The only water available was the water that came from the big well that sat in the front yard. We would pump the water up to use it. I didn't like well water because it had a funny taste. It didn't taste the same as the water at my house which ran from the faucet.

Maybe the water from my faucet tasted funny to my island family when they visited our house. I was also afraid of the outhouse, especially at night when it was pitch black and there was no electricity. It didn't look anything like bathrooms in the city of Charleston and it was usually outside in the back of the house. Wouldn't you be just a little scared too? To my family members and other people who lived there, it was a part of the experience and culture at the time. I don't think that they gave it a second thought. Outhouses certainly wasn't anything new. Enslaved people used them in groups on different plantations in Charleston.

McLeod Plantation   © GJFC, Inc. 9/2018

This small building is an outhouse located at McLeod Plantation in Charleston. It has six toilets in this small space for enslaved people to use. If you look carefully at the picture above you can see one of them.

Growing up, I had family members who taught me how to go out on the water for crabs. I learned how to shrimp and how to throw a net with chicken meat attached to bring the crabs into the net. It was a way of life and survival for many people in the sea islands. It was a business for many who sold the seafood they caught throughout the islands and on the street corners and markets. A lot of families had "crab cracks" or just plain old good times sitting around the table "eatin crabs wid da famly" until you couldn't' place another crab shell on top of the high mound of empty shells. Okra soup, red rice, smoked neckbones and smothered everything with rice, including rice and eggs for breakfast; blackeyed peas and rice, or hoppin' johns as everyone called it every New Year's Day. We loved eating shrimp n' grits and sweet yams with marshmallows on top that would make you bite off a finger. We ate collard greens, fish, cabbage, stewed tomatoes and bread pudding, which was my Dad's favorite. The stories and bonding that took place over those meals were extra special and they created memories and traditions that are shared from one generation to the next. We still cook many of these meals today especially around the holidays. It was all Gullah Geechee Good!

© GJFC, Inc. 9/2018

Above is Uncle Arnold's "Poor People's Food" (*left*, Recipe from Grandma Leezie) and my shrimp dish ready for rice or grits. (*right*, Recipe passed from Uncle Paul)

I learned a lot even though I didn't know it at the time. I was just a little girl growing up like you and everybody else. Our parents made sure that we were rich in love and culture and family values. At the time, it didn't necessarily seem special, it just seemed normal. What I know now is that the name, Gullah Geechee, is so much more than a name. Gullah Geechee is about a people, a life experience and a rich heritage of Africanism maintained by a people dwelling on the coastal shorelines of the Southeastern corridor. It's about the journey of my ancestors and maybe some of your ancestors who were forcibly brought across the Atlantic Ocean and who touched the grounds of cities like Charleston, eventually living throughout sea islands such as Sandy Island, Johns Island, James Island, Daniel Island, St. Helena, Amelia Island and Beaufort to name a few.

It's about those ancestors who walked the winding roads in the islands and who toiled in those plantation fields. It's about elders and ancestors who stayed strong to survive for their families, for me and for you. It's about those ancestors who we lost and whose lives and contributions we must respect, whether we remember or knew them individually or not. It is about elders and ancestors who used ingenuity and innovation to make sure that we got what we needed even if it wasn't enough or what we wanted at the time. It's about those ancestors who fought, who stood up, who ran when it was the wiser decision, who hid those in need of a shield, who created in spite of, who became educated because of and who passed the blueprint of ingenuity and survivalist in our DNA. It is about going back, recognizing and respecting their contributions and bringing it forward.

So, where am I from?

I am from Africa via Charleston, Johns Island, James Island and Wadmalaw Island. I am proud to be called a Gullah Geechee. It means I have great roots; ….and **your root is your foundation**.

© GJFC, Inc. 9/2018

Written by this Gullah Geechee Woman

Angel Harriott is Founder of Global Journey for Children, Inc. The mission is to promote cultural competency. Support this organization at ajourneyforchildren.org

Ode to the Ancestors

You cannot ask me to forget

It is in my blood

You cannot expect me not to want to know

It is in my soul

You cannot keep their memories away from me

They are in my heart.

Sya   11/2018

Sankofa is everywhere to remind us to go back and fetch our history.

Sacred Burial Site across from McLeod Plantation   © GJFC, Inc. – Photo by C. Harriott 9/2018

This burial site was discovered on James Island, SC when the land was about to be developed. It is now considered a sacred burial site. The Sankofa symbol of the bird acknowledges, "going back to fetch history". The city is now determining how to pay homage to this land and ancestors who were buried here so many years ago.

REFERENCES

Oral Interviews

Books:
Cross, Wilbur; Gullah Culture in America
Nathaniel Johnson; Grass Roots: African Origins of an American Art
Pollitzer, Wiliam S.; The Gullah People and Their African Heritage

Websites:
https://nmaahc.si.edu/object/nmaahc_2013.57.
https://en.wikipedia.org/wiki/American_Revolutionary_War
https://www.tolerance.org/classroom-resources/texts/hard-history/cabin-from-point-of-pines-plantation.

THIS PAGE IS INTENTIONALLY LEFT BLANK